Fall and Winter Wild Bird Feed Sale

Book 2 of the NAIWBS
Marketing Brief Series

**This Marketing Brief
is designed to
increase sales
and
improve operations
of your
Wild Bird Food Sale**

National Association of Independent Wild Bird Stores

Developed for
NAIWBS by
John F. Gardner

Copyright Notice

Legal Notices

THE OPTIONS AVAILABLE FOR THE
WILD BIRD FEED SALE

A Wild Bird Feed Sale is designed to reward your customers for feeding the birds using your brand or a quality brand of wild bird feed. It also puts you on par with other feed retailers who tend to have this kind of sale in the fall. Many suppliers do this to unload 'old crop' feed so that storage is empty to accept new crop. You need to avoid this concept and emphasize the features and benefits of your brand of feed.

Position your feed sale as a benefit to loyal customers who have traded with you over the year. This is a way to say 'thank you' and help them prepare for the up coming feeding season.

The sale can be done in two ways:

1. Pre-ordering, prepay, pickup specific day Sale.

With this system you mail your customers a letter and an order form advising them that you are holding a sale and all wild bird feed will be discounted some percent *(up to you)* for a very limited time. *(I suggest no more than a week or two at the most. I also suggest you limit the number of pounds any household can buy. This reduces your loss of future sales at full price.)* Your customers fill out the order form, attach a check, mail it back to you and then prepare to come in during a certain period to pickup their feed. With this system you need to bring in sufficient feed to meet pre-orders plus some for walk-ins. We have found that this is a good sale to have because it comes and goes in a fixed period of time and your liability is limited as to time, price and profit.

2. Pre-order, prepay, draw as needed Sale.

With this system, again you send out a letter and order form. However, with this system you allow the customer to pickup the feed any time over a fixed period *(say October through January)* from the on-going inventory in your store. With this sale, the customer gets a discount, while you get the money in advance plus the extra benefit of the customer coming into your store periodically to pickup feed, and maybe buy something else. This is a good system. Again, I suggest you limit the amount *(pounds)* any one household can buy under this program. The disadvantage of this program is that the price of feed could go up between the time the customer buys it and the time he or she picks up the feed. A price increase would result in a much lower margin than you anticipated. If the price of feed goes down then your margin is higher *(You get to play the odds)*.

SECTION ONE

Pre Order
Pre Pay
Pick Up Day of Sale

SECTION ONE

TABLE OF CONTENTS:

Advertising and Marketing Schedule
A week by week schedule of events and activities you need to do in order to have a successful Wild Bird Feed Sale.

Delivery, Storage and Operating Procedures
Things you want to think about to make your sale run smoothly.

Procedures for a specific day pick up program
Ideas and suggestions for sale operations.

Things to check prior to the sale
Review of key elements for sale activities.

SCHEDULE OF ACTIVITIES
Pick Up Day of Sale Program

 Here is a listing of activities by date that you should follow when preparing for your Wild Bird Feed Sale. Be sure to allow sufficient time for each activity, especially for your mail to be delivered.

☐ **Eight weeks before your Sale**

Decide if you are going to hold a week long sale, or a weekend (Sat-Sun) sale. Prepare your order form and mailer. Define your product line, price, closing date for ordering, and the procedures that you will use for pickups.

☐ **Seven weeks before your Sale**

Print mailer, prepare address labels from your customer base, and sort for bulk mailing.

☐ **Six weeks before your Sale**

Your flyer is mailed to your customer list. Experience has shown that an order form mailer is the most successful procedure. Make use of every mailing list that you have or can borrow.

☐ **Five weeks before your Sale**

Run newspaper advertisements announcing your sale and send press releases announcing the fall feeding season, include your sale information.

☐ **Four weeks before your Sale**

Circulate supplemental press releases. Also, give talks to garden clubs, civic groups and local TV programs.

❏ **Three weeks before your Sale**

Run a newspaper ad announcing the closing date is coming up and orders should be sent in immediately. Stimulate your customers to act at once.

❏ **Fifteen days before your Sale**

Compile orders and make up a master order. It helps to keep a running total of orders. It makes the compiling job easier.

❏ **Ten working days before your Sale**

Call your feed order into your supplier. On the day you place your order with your feed supplier be sure to tell them that this order is for a special feed sale and the feed must be delivered one or two days before your sale. This may require a change in their delivery day. If the feed supplier has sufficient time in advance this should not be a problem.

❏ **Eight days before your sale or sooner**

Line up helpers to off load the feed when it comes into your store. The supplier should give you plenty of notice. The driver may or may not assist, his main job is to pull the feed to the rear of the truck so you and your helpers can off load the feed.

❏ **Five days before the close of your sale**

Send out a postcard or run an ad reminding your customers of the pickup procedures. Remember this is a short term marketing program and should not run more than one or two weeks.

Feed delivery to your location:

You should arrange for your feed to be delivered to your store or storage location sometime during the <u>several days</u> before your pick up sale day. You do not want to be caught with a major marketing program going and no feed. Also, keep in mind that your customers may pre-order for pickup more feed than you can store. In this case you will need to rent a truck to store the extra feed or come up with some kind of on or off site storage.

REMINDER: Under no circumstances should you ever ask the truck driver to pull the trailer off of the blacktop or roadway. We have seen to many trailers sink up to the axle on grass or soft areas. If the trailer sinks and it was at your direction, you will have to pay the tow truck to pull the trailer out.

If you have special delivery requirements be sure to let your feed supplier know early in the process so that they can work with you to make the Sale run as smoothly as possible.

Unloading the seed:

Unloading the feed and storage are going to be your responsibility. We suggest that you try to plan on having one person available for each ton of feed to be off loaded. In addition, be sure that someone has the responsibility to direct the driver into the off loading area and check the delivery slip as the feed is off loaded. By now you have a system worked out with your feed supplier so this unloading of an extra large order of feed should be relatively simple. *Something worth planning for: 10,000 pounds of feed makes a pile approximately 10 feet by 10 feet by 8 feet high, unsorted.*

Storage:

Stores who do not have adequate storage for their feed have several options.

1. It is often possible to put the feed in a small storage truck rented from UHaul or Ryder until the sale is over. This eats into your profits so be careful.

2. If your volume exceeds 35,000 pounds it may be possible to convince the feed supplier to let the trailer remain at your site for the sale. There is usually an additional charge for this service when it is available. But, it does turn your sale into a real Sale.

3. I strongly recommend that as you unload the seed you sort it by product. Then on the day of the sale your helpers will have little or no problem filling the customers order.

Procedures the day of the sale:

You will need additional help on the weekends of your sale. How many you will need depends on the amount of feed you have sold. I would think you would need the following people on the weekend of your sale.

One person to greet your customers and explain the procedure. They will also answer questions and wait on customers.

One person to process orders at the checkout counter. They should be well versed on prices and on the computer.

One or more strong person to handle and load the bags of feed into the customers car.

The Operating Process:

The customer starts the process by sending back the order form with a check. You then verify the order and note the check number on the form to indicate payment has been made. You then file the order form in an alphabetical file.

On the weekend of your sale the customer comes into the store and is met by a person who explains the procedure. The customer is then invited to look around the store or go directly to the check out counter for feed order processing.

At the checkout counter the order is pulled from the alphabetical file and verified. The verified order is given to the customer, who then drives to a predetermined pickup location, presents a verified order form to a helper, who in turn loads the feed into the customers car. The helper keeps the order for future cross checking.

You will need to create some kind of a system or modify this system to meet your particular store layout, location, amount of feed sold, and available help. During the weekdays the process is not complicated because of the limited number of people who will pickup their feed. However, on the weekend it is a different story. Plan Ahead.

Don't forget to cross sell other products during this sale. Suet, Feeders, Baffles, Poles, Books, etc.

Things to check prior to the day of your sale:

(For a Weekend Sale)

 Review the parking, pickup, traffic patterns and procedures you will be using during the sale. Consider the various possibilities and anticipate any problems. Review each step of the process with any extra help you are bringing in for the sale.

Be sure you have your bird feed sorted into easily identified product piles. Depending on how much you have sold you may need to put extra pallets of feed out on the sidewalk with the person loading the customers cars.

Have plenty of change available for cash payments. Be sure you have <u>customer mailing list sign-up forms available</u> and <u>use them</u>.

Consider having coffee, cookies, hot chocolate, etc. for your customers. Remember, a Bird Feed Truckload Sale should be a fun time for your customers and helpers. Make it a pleasant experience.

SECTION TWO

Pre Order
Pre Pay
Pick Up as Needed Sale

SECTION TWO
Pick up seed as needed

TABLE OF CONTENTS:

Advertising and Marketing Schedule
A week by week schedule of events and activities you need to do in order to have a successful Wild Bird Feed Sale.

Storage and Operating Procedures
Things you want to think about to make your sale run smoothly.

Things to check prior to the sale
Review of key elements for sale activities.

SCHEDULE OF ACTIVITIES
Pick up Seed as Needed Program

Here is a listing of activities by date that you should follow when preparing for your Bird Feed Sale. Be sure to allow sufficient time for each activity, especially for your mailings to be delivered.

❑ **Eight weeks before your Sale**
Prepare your order form and mailer. Define your product line, price, closing date for ordering, and the procedures that you will use for customer pick up over the time period allocated (Oct.-Dec.).

❑ **Seven weeks before your Sale**
Print mailer, prepare address labels from your customer base, and sort for bulk mailing.

❑ **Six weeks before your Sale**
Your flyer is mailed to your customer list. Experience has shown that an order form mailer is the most successful procedure. Make use of every mailing list that you have or can borrow.

❑ **Five weeks before your Sale**
Run newspaper advertisements announcing your sale and send press releases announcing the fall feeding season, include your sale information.

❑ **Four weeks before your Sale**
Circulate supplemental press releases. Also, give talks to garden clubs, civic groups and local TV programs civic groups and local TV programs.

❑ **Three weeks before your Sale**

Run a newspaper ad announcing the closing date is coming up and orders should be sent in immediately. Stimulate your customers to act at once.

❑ **Fifteen days before your Sale**

Compile orders and make up a master list. It helps to keep a running total of orders. It makes the compiling job easier. If you are using the a point of sale computer program, enter the order as a lay-away order.

❑ **Ten working days before your Sale**

You will not have to call an order into your supplier because your customers will draw their seed from your ongoing inventory stockpiles.

❑ **Five days before the close of your sale**

Send out a postcard or run an ad reminding your customers of the pickup procedures. Remember this is a short term marketing program and should not run more than one or two weeks.

The Operating Process:

The customer starts the process by sending back the order form with a check. You then verify the order and note the check number on the form to indicate payment has been made. You then file the order form in an alphabetical file.

Because the customer will pull the seed from existing inventory the process stops at this point until such time as the customer comes in and asks for their seed.

When the customer comes in to pick up their seed you can use your point of sale program to process the order as a draw from layaway. If you are not using a computerised point of sale program then you need to develop a card system for tracking the draw down. (*If you are doing the process with cards you will have to manually adjust your inventory to account for the draw down.*)

Remember, use all of your 'cross selling' skills each time the customer comes in to pick up pre-ordered seed. Two weeks before the program runs out send a postcard to customers telling them they must pick up the balance of their order by a certain date.

Again you will need to create some kind of a system or modify this system to meet your particular store layout, location, amount of feed sold, and computer system in operation.

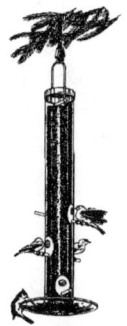

Second Reminder;

Don't forget to cross sell other products during this sale. Suet, Feeders, Baffles, Poles, Books, etc.

SECTION THREE:

Ordering procedures to increase sales
Mail order and phone order.

Marketing Helps
To increase sales

Product Descriptions
Something you should be proud to offer your community.

Advertising and Marketing Aids
To help increase sales.

Some ordering procedures that may help you increase sales: *(Good for either type sale)*

THE BASIC METHOD:
Orders taken through the mail

Most orders will come in by mail, accompanied by a check for the full amount of the order. This is a result of your customer mailing and order form. Hand out or mail out, but <u>circulate as many order forms as possible</u>.

All mail order forms should be marked, checked for accuracy and the correct amount of money. Check numbers should be marked on the order form as a record of payment. The order forms should be sorted into alphabetical order, and filed as prepaid orders. *(Again, this procedure can be used with either kind of sale).* Remember, mail orders and distribution of order forms are the most successful way of promoting your Wild Bird Feed Sale.

TO INCREASE SALES

Consider taking orders over the phone in response to direct mail, newspaper or radio advertising

Some stores have found that taking orders over the phone is a good idea. Money for these phone orders can be charged to a credit card, they can be collected the day of the sale or when the customer first comes in for a pickup of feed.

Phone orders should be taken on an order form. Do not get sloppy and jot them down on a note pad. Keep good records at all times. These orders should reflect if the person is on your mailing list or not. If they are no, be sure they do get on the mailing list so you can do later mailings and invitations to make the person a regular customer.

It is important that the person calling in an order be told of the sales period and the pickup procedure that you have in place for this sale.

SUMMARY:

Holding a Wild Bird Feed Sale can be fun, exciting, and profitable. I Hope this manual is a help.

Additional
Sales
Support

MARKETING HELP

Product Description Sheet
Sample Letter
Sample Order Form

Because you have purchased this Marketing Manual
you are given permission to use any
of the graphics in preparing for your local
Wild Bird seed sale.

PRODUCT DESCRIPTIONS
(Modify to match your product offerings)

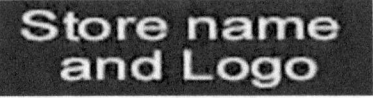

Blends

You must offer a truly high quality bird feed mix for your customers convenience. When we held a sale we were able to tell customer that each had been researched and developed for over 30 years. These mixes were guaranteed to attract all of the 28 common feeder birds that come to yards and gardens. Check with your supplier for any unique or special features.

A few examples of descriptions:

Deluxe Blend :
This is a combination of black oil sunflower feed, black striped sunflower feed, peanut splits, safflower feed and white proso millet. With 30% sunflower feed and no waste ingredients, this is truly a quality blend.

Special Blend :
No corn is what makes this blend special. It's new formulation will be a combination of black oil sunflower feed, safflower feed, peanut splits, white proso millet, and canary feed. This mix has over 40% sunflower, and will attract a wide variety of backyard feeder birds.

Custom Blend :
Better than most premium blends offered by our competition, and priced to compete at the economy level. However, this is not an economy blend, this is a quality product.

> You might want to
> consider some of these
> products in your offering.

Black Oil Sunflower: Truly the most attractive feed to the widest variety of feed eating birds. Research at the Cornell Lab of Ornithology has shown that birds prefer Black Oil Sunflower 2 to 1 over other sunflower seeds. Our Black Oil sunflower seeds are required to be cleaned, recleaned and de-sticked before being packaged and shipped to your store.

Nyjer Seed: Goldfinches, Pine Siskins, Redpolls, House Finches and Purple Finches are just a few of the birds that relish Nyjer (Thistle) feed. Nyjer feed is grown in Ethiopia and/or India, It is sterilized in USDA supervised plants prior to release in the US. We pride ourselves on the freshness and quality of our Niger feed.

Safflower Seed: This seed's claim to fame is that squirrels don't like it. Safflower is a favorite of Northern Cardinals, Mourning Doves and Titmice. This pure white feed is grown in California, Canada, Arizona and other states in the Midwest. Off coloring sometimes occurs when the growing season is particularly wet. This off coloring has no effect on the popularity of the feed.

White Proso Millet: White millet is primarily known as a feed for ground feeders. Everything from Mourning Doves to Sparrows like white proso millet. It is the second most popular wild bird food ingredient.

Cracked Corn: This is another of the ground feeding birds choices. Almost 90 different wild birds will eat cracked corn, including the Northern Cardinal. Our corn is steel cut and graded to medium size.

Split Peanuts: This is a relatively new ingredient used in bird feed formulations. It has replaced peanut hearts in many of the better feed mixes. Peanut splits are extremely attractive to Titmice, Chickadees, Blue Jays and White Throated Sparrows. Peanut Splits are a tremendous addition to anyone's backyard feeding program.

Black Striped Sunflower: This is not as popular as the black oil feed, however, it is still very attractive to the larger feed eating birds - especially Grosbeaks and Cardinals.

Suet Cakes: Birds use suet as a substitute for insect larvae, eggs and pupa. We recommend **suet** cakes that are made only from the hard, white fat found around the kidneys of beef cattle. In addition, you don't have to worry about suet cakes going rancid. All of the impurities are removed during processing. Suet is a very popular food for all Woodpeckers, as well as, Chickadees and other clinging birds.

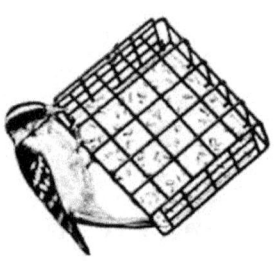

Speciality Feed Products:
There are many specialty blends available, such as Woodpecker mix and Cardinal mix. Ask your suppliers sales person about these blends.

Sample Letter - Pick up Specific Dates
Modify to reflect the program you are using

Your address, phone number, hours and
map to your store go here

Dear Customer:

We have joined together with our seed supplier to bring you a special opportunity. In appreciation of your loyal support of our store, we are giving you an opportunity to buy your bird feed at special reduced prices.

Through a program of new crop bulk buying, quality control, pre-ordering and cooperative efforts we can offer you our very high quality, nutritious Wild Bird feed at great savings.

During the period of October xx AND xx, we will hold our annual Bird Feed Sale. In order to insure sufficient feed, we ask that you pre-order, using the enclosed order form. Order forms should be returned to us on or before xxxxxxxxxx so that we can ensure your feed arrives by October xxxx. Your feed will be available and must be picked up October xxxx, here at the store to take advantage of these special prices.

We Appreciate your support of our efforts to bring quality birding products to our community, and hope that you will continue to support our store. Again, we appreciate your patronage and this sale is our way of saying 'Thank You'.

Sincerely,

Store name and Logo

Are you on our
Mailing list?_____
Phone #_____

THIS IS YOUR ORDER FORM:

Your Name:_____

Your Address:_____

Your City, Zip:_____

Quantity Ordered	Product:	Special price per bag	Your Sub Total:
_____	25 lb. Black Oil Sunflower...........	_____	_____
_____	50 lb. Black Oil Sunflower...........	_____	_____
_____	20 lb. Deluxe Mix........................	_____	_____
_____	40 lb. Deluxe Mix........................	_____	_____
_____	20 lb. Special Mix	_____	_____
_____	40 lb. Special Mix	_____	_____
_____	25 lb. Cracked Corn.....................	_____	_____
_____	25 lb. White Proso Millet.............	_____	_____
_____	5 lb. Sunflower Chips...................	_____	_____
_____	20 lb. Sunflower Chips..................	_____	_____
_____	5 lb. Peanut Splits.........................	_____	_____
_____	20 lb. Peanut Splits.......................	_____	_____
_____	5 lb. Safflower Seed......................	_____	_____
_____	20 lb. Safflower Seed.....................	_____	_____
_____	5 lb. Nyjer (Thistle) Seed.............	_____	_____
_____	20 lb. Nyjer (Thistle) Seed.............	_____	_____

Orders limited to a total of xxx pounds of seed.

Please Send or Bring
Order Form To:

xxxxxxxxxxxxxxxxxx
xxxxxxxxxxxxxxxxxx
xxxxxxxxxxxxxxxxxx

Return by: xxxxxxx

Total $ .... _____
Plus Tax   .... _____

Total Due .. ... _____

Please attach your check

Use the following pages to record any successes, any changes or modification you might need to make for your next "Wildbird Feed Sale"

_____

_____

_____

_____

_____

_____

_____

_____

_____

_____

_____

_____

_____

_____

_____

_____

 **Marketing Brief**

The Series:

1. Gearing up for Greater Sales

150 pages of help during times when things need a boost.
Available from Amazon

2. Fall and Winter Wild Bird Feed Sale

Based on 41 years of experience in holding wild bird feed sales - Available from Amazon

3. Newspaper Advertising Workbook

Don't start advertising until after you read this manual.
Scheduled Publication in Early March 2016

4. Location, Location, Location

How the big boys do it.
Pending Publication in Mid-March 2016

5. The Wilkerson Formula

How to make $9,000 on a weekend
Pending Publication near the end of March 2016